The Ultimate Casserole Cookbook

Incredible Casserole Dishes You'd Love

BY: SOPHIA FREEMAN

© 2020 Sophia Freeman All Rights Reserved

COPYRIGHTED

Liability

This publication is meant as an informational tool. The individual purchaser accepts all liability if damages occur because of following the directions or guidelines set out in this publication. The Author bears no responsibility for reparations caused by the misuse or misinterpretation of the content.

Copyright

The content of this publication is solely for entertainment purposes and is meant to be purchased by one individual. Permission is not given to any individual who copies, sells or distributes parts or the whole of this publication unless it is explicitly given by the Author in writing.

Table of Contents

Introduction 7

Ham Hash Brown Casserole 10

Asparagus, Mushroom Chicken Casserole 13

Cheesy Broccoli Casserole 17

Spaghetti Squash Casserole 21

Asparagus Casserole 25

Reuben Casserole 29

Sloppy Joe Casserole 33

Beef Enchilada Casserole 37

Eggplant Parmesan Casserole 42

Tex-Mex Casserole 46

Cheesy Broccoli Rice Casserole 50

Squash Casserole 54

Zucchini Casserole 58

Baked Chicken Spaghetti Squash 61

Eggplant Casserole 65

Breakfast Casserole 69

Oatmeal Casserole 72

Shrimp Casserole 75

Turkey Broccoli Casserole 78

Cauliflower Casserole 82

Green Bean Casserole 85

Herbed Garlic Potato Casserole 88

Ham Egg Casserole 91

Zucchini Pizza Casserole 94

Turkey Zucchini Lasagna 98

Apple Sweet Potato Casserole 102

Cheesy Zucchini Frittata 105

Cheese Mushroom Casserole 108

Polenta Lasagna 112

Green Bean Casserole 116

Potato Sausage Casserole 119

Mexican Beef Bake 122

Chicken Cordon Bleu Casserole 126

Salmon Casserole 130

Turkey Rice Casserole 133

Tuna Casserole 137

Tuna Pasta Casserole 141

Baked Penne 144

Cheesy Turkey Casserole 148

Chicken Strata 151

Chicken Cashew Casserole 154

Baked Tomato Squash 158

Burger Casserole 162

Pizza Casserole 166

Chicken Curry Casserole 170

Pasta Casserole 173

Sausage Sweet Potato Casserole 177

Hash Brown Baked Eggs 181

Conclusion 184

About the Author 185

Author's Afterthoughts 187

Introduction

Many people will agree: casseroles are a great idea whenever there's an occasion and you don't want to spend too much time, effort and money.

Casseroles are not only filling and delicious, they're also versatile dishes that can involve a wide array of ingredients—meat, poultry, vegetables, herbs, spices, sauces, gravies, cheeses and so on.

The term "casserole" is rooted from the French word "casse", which means pan. A casserole refers to a deep pan that can be used either in the oven for baking or for serving.

Casseroles are said to have originated in ancient Greece. In the 1870s, the casserole has found its way to other parts of the world.

In the 1950s, it has become a famous dish in the United States, following the introduction of metal cookware that's lighter and easier to use.

In Europe and the United States, casseroles are typically made with ground meat or chicken, chopped or sliced vegetables, and a type of binder. Popular options for binders are pasta, potatoes, and flour. More often than not, casseroles are topped with melted cheese. In some recipes, juices, water, cider, tomato sauce and other cooking liquids are added to create a more flavorful result.

Most people prefer to serve the casserole as main course, given that it's not only delicious but also quite filling; however, there are also those who prefer to serve the casserole as a side dish, adding a slice of the dish to a plated main course.

Some of the most popular casseroles all over the world include:

- Shepherd's pie (United Kingdom)
- Lancashire hotpot (England)
- Ragout, cassoulet (France)
- Green bean casserole (US)
- Carbonnade (Belgium)

In this book, you'll find many savory casserole recipes that make use of different ingredients. Whatever it is you are craving for, for sure you will find the casserole dish to satisfy your taste buds. You'll also find something suitable for the occasion that you are preparing for.

Ham Hash Brown Casserole

This is the kind of casserole that both kids and adults will enjoy. Another thing to love about it is that it's very easy to prepare and won't require too much effort in the kitchen.

Serving Size: 16

Preparation Cooking Time: an hour and 30 minutes

Ingredients:

- Cooking spray
- ¼ cup all-purpose flour
- 4 cups milk, divided
- 1 cup mozzarella cheese, shredded
- 1 cup cheddar cheese, shredded
- Pepper to taste
- 2 cups deli ham, sliced into cubes
- 3 cups peas
- 10 cups hash browns, shredded

Instructions:

1. Preheat your oven to 375 degrees F.

2. Coat your baking pan with oil.

3. Combine the flour and ½ cup milk in a bowl.

4. Pour the remaining milk into a pan over medium heat and simmer for 2 minutes while stirring.

5. Stir in the flour mixture.

6. Simmer for 5 minutes.

7. Turn off the heat.

8. Stir in the mozzarella and cheddar.

9. Season with the pepper.

10. Mix the ham, peas and hash browns in a bowl.

11. Pour the mixture into a baking pan.

12. Cover with the foil and bake for 50 minutes.

13. Remove the foil and bake for 3 to 5 minutes or until the surface has turned golden.

Nutrients per Serving:

- Calories 192
- Fat 7 g
- Saturated fat 3.6 g
- Carbohydrates 21.1 g
- Fiber 2.2 g
- Protein 11.4 g
- Cholesterol 25 mg
- Sugars 4 g
- Sodium 372 mg
- Potassium 396 mg

Asparagus, Mushroom Chicken Casserole

As you know, chicken and mushroom go well together. But what you probably didn't know is that a third ingredient, asparagus can make this combination even more delicious. In this casserole, we load up the pan with plenty mushrooms, asparagus, shredded chicken and brown rice, all topped with savory cheese sauce.

Serving Size: 6

Preparation Cooking Time: 40 minutes

Ingredients:

- 2 tablespoons olive oil
- 1 cup yellow onion, chopped
- 16 oz. button mushrooms
- 3 tablespoons all-purpose flour
- 2 ½ cups milk
- 2 teaspoons fresh tarragon leaves, chopped
- Salt to taste
- ½ cup Parmesan cheese, grated and divided
- 2 cups cooked brown rice
- 2 cups chicken breast fillet, cooked and shredded
- 1 lb. asparagus spears, sliced
- 1 ½ teaspoons olive oil
- ¼ cup whole-wheat panko breadcrumbs

Instructions:

1. Preheat your oven to 375 degrees F.

2. Pour 2 tablespoons oil in a pan over medium heat.

3. Cook the onion and mushrooms for 10 minutes.

4. Stir in the flour and milk.

5. Simmer around 2 minutes or until the liquid has thickened.

6. Add the tarragon and salt.

7. Stir in half of the Parmesan cheese.

8. Add the rice, chicken and asparagus.

9. Turn off the heat.

10. Combine the remaining Parmesan cheese, remaining olive oil and breadcrumbs in a bowl.

11. Spread this mixture on top of the pan.

12. Transfer the pan to the oven and bake for 15 minutes.

Nutrients per Serving:

- Calories 329
- Fat 12.5 g
- Saturated fat 4.2 g
- Carbohydrates 29.6 g
- Fiber 3.7 g
- Protein 26 g
- Cholesterol 56 mg
- Sugars 9 g
- Sodium 413 mg
- Potassium 745 mg

Cheesy Broccoli Casserole

So, your friends are coming over and you don't know what to prepare for lunch or dinner. You check your kitchen and you find almost nothing but cheese and broccoli. Here's what you can do—cheesy broccoli casserole that's sure to be a big hit.

Serving Size: 8

Preparation Cooking Time: 50 minutes

Ingredients:

- 1 ½ pounds broccoli florets
- 2 tablespoons olive oil
- 1 onion, chopped
- 2 cloves garlic, crushed and minced
- 4 oz. low-fat cream cheese
- 1 ½ cups cheddar cheese, shredded
- ½ cup sour cream
- Salt and pepper to taste

Instructions:

1. Preheat your oven to 350 degrees F.

2. Fill your pot with an inch of the water and put a steamer basket inside.

3. Steam the broccoli for 5 minutes.

4. Chop coarsely.

5. Pour the oil into a pan over medium heat.

6. Cook the onion for 3 minutes.

7. Add the garlic.

8. Reduce heat and cook the garlic for 5 minutes.

9. Turn off the stove and transfer the onion and garlic mixture in a bowl.

10. Add to the onion mixture the cream cheese, 1 cup cheddar and sour cream.

11. Season with the salt and pepper.

12. Mix well.

13. Stir in the steamed broccoli.

14. Pour the mixture into a baking pan.

15. Top with the remaining cheddar.

16. Bake in the oven for 25 minutes.

17. Let it cool around 10 minutes before slicing and serving.

Nutrients per Serving:

- Calories 179
- Fat 14.8 g
- Saturated fat 6.8 g
- Carbohydrates 5.2 g
- Fiber 0.7 g
- Protein 7.3 g
- Cholesterol 37 mg
- Sugars 2 g
- Sodium 339 mg
- Potassium 126 mg

Spaghetti Squash Casserole

Among all the dishes you can make with spaghetti squash, this will most likely become your favorite. You're going to love how the tender yet crunchy strands of spaghetti squash complement perfectly with creamy sauce and melted cheese. And let's not forget, this is a low-carb and low-calorie alternative to the usual pasta.

Serving Size: 4

Preparation Cooking Time: 40 minutes

Ingredients:

- 1 spaghetti squash, sliced in half lengthwise
- 2 tablespoons water
- 1 lb. lean ground beef
- 2 cloves garlic, crushed and minced
- 1 shallot, chopped
- Salt and pepper to taste
- 1 ½ teaspoons Italian seasoning
- 52 oz. canned crushed tomatoes
- 1 cup fontina cheese, shredded
- Fresh basil leaves

Instructions:

1. Preheat your oven to 400 degrees F.

2. Add the squash in a microwave-safe pan.

3. Pour in the water.

4. Microwave on high for 10 minutes.

5. In pan over medium heat, cook the ground beef for 5 minutes.

6. Stir in the garlic and shallot.

7. Sprinkle with the salt, pepper and Italian seasoning.

8. Cook while stirring for 1 minute.

9. Add the tomatoes.

10. Bring to a boil. Reduce heat and simmer.

11. Scrape the flesh using a fork.

12. Add to the pan and stir.

13. Sprinkle the cheese on top.

14. Bake in the oven for 15 minutes.

15. Garnish with the fresh basil leaves and serve.

Nutrients per Serving:

- Calories 470
- Fat 19.8 g
- Saturated fat 9.4 g
- Carbohydrates 27.5 g
- Fiber 7.1 g
- Protein 42.9 g
- Cholesterol 118 mg
- Sugars 13 g
- Sodium 719 mg
- Potassium 1299 mg

Asparagus Casserole

In this recipe, we pour creamy cheese sauce and sprinkle crunchy breadcrumbs on top of fresh asparagus spears. This dish is loaded with cheesy and savory flavors that you love. Make sure that you blanch the asparagus and not overcook it so that they'd still have the bright green color that make this dish look more appetizing.

Serving Size: 10

Preparation Cooking Time: 45 minutes

Ingredients:

- 3 tablespoons butter, divided
- ½ cup panko breadcrumbs
- 3 lb. asparagus spears, trimmed and sliced
- 1 tablespoon garlic, chopped
- 2 tablespoons all-purpose flour
- 2 cups whole milk
- Salt to taste
- ½ cup mozzarella cheese, shredded
- 5 oz. cream cheese

Instructions:

1. Preheat your oven to 450 degrees F.

2. Melt 1 tablespoon butter in a saucepan over medium heat.

3. Remove from heat.

4. Stir in the breadcrumbs and set aside.

5. Prepare a bowl filled with water near the stove.

6. Add ice cubes to the bowl.

7. Boil a pot of water.

8. Blanch the asparagus for 1 minute.

9. Plunge the asparagus in the bowl of ice water.

10. Let stand for 5 to 6 minutes. Drain.

11. Spread the blanched asparagus on a baking pan.

12. Put the pot back to the stove.

13. Add the remaining butter.

14. Cook the garlic for 1 minute.

15. Stir in the flour and milk.

16. Bring to a boil.

17. Reduce heat and simmer while stirring until the mixture has thickened.

18. Remove from heat.

19. Stir in the remaining ingredients.

20. Pour this mixture on top of the asparagus.

21. Coat evenly.

22. Sprinkle with the breadcrumb mixture.

23. Bake in the oven for 15 minutes.

Nutrients per Serving:

- Calories 179
- Fat 11.5 g
- Saturated fat 6.6 g
- Carbohydrates 12.8 g
- Fiber 2.7 g
- Protein 7.4 g
- Cholesterol 32 mg
- Sugars 5 g
- Sodium 360 mg
- Potassium 380 mg

Reuben Casserole

Love Reuben sandwich? Then for sure, you'd love this casserole version of the world-famous sandwich but with fewer calories and less sodium. Giving the casserole extra flavor are the deli turkey and vinegar, which stand in place of corned beef and sauerkraut.

Serving Size: 6

Preparation Cooking Time: 40 minutes

Ingredients:

- Cooking spray
- 3 tablespoons olive oil, divided
- 1 cup yellow onion, chopped
- 5 cups green cabbage, sliced very thinly
- Salt to taste
- 2 tablespoons cider vinegar
- 1 ¼ cups Swiss cheese, shredded
- 2 tablespoons dill pickle, chopped
- ¼ lb. deli turkey, chopped
- ¼ cup light mayonnaise
- 2 tablespoons low-sodium ketchup
- 3 slices rye bread, sliced into small cubes

Instructions:

1. Preheat your oven to 350 degrees F.

2. Spray your baking pan with oil.

3. Pour a tablespoon oil in a pan over medium heat.

4. Add the onion, cabbage and salt.

5. Cook for 5 minutes.

6. Add the vinegar and turn off the heat.

7. Pour the mixture into the baking pan.

8. Spread half of the cheese on top, and then the pickled dill and then the turkey.

9. In a bowl, combine the mayo and ketchup.

10. Spread on top of the turkey.

11. Sprinkle the bread on top.

12. Drizzle with the remaining olive oil.

13. Top with the remaining cheese.

14. Bake in the oven for 20 minutes.

Nutrients per Serving:

- Calories 338
- Fat 23.9 g
- Saturated fat 6.7 g
- Carbohydrates 17 g
- Fiber 3 g
- Protein 14 g
- Cholesterol 7 mg
- Sugars 6 g
- Sodium 493 mg
- Potassium 243 mg

Sloppy Joe Casserole

This Sloppy Joe casserole recipe won't only get your kids excited but will also allow you to sneak in veggies to their meal without them noticing! Plus, this is easy to prepare too.

Serving Size: 6

Preparation Cooking Time: 30 minutes

Ingredients:

- 10 oz. elbow noodles
- 1 tablespoon vegetable oil
- 1 lb. ground turkey
- 2 cups onions, chopped
- 5 cloves garlic, crushed and minced
- 2 cups red bell peppers, chopped
- 1 cup carrots, grated
- 2 ½ cups cauliflower rice
- 15 oz. canned tomato sauce
- 1 ½ tablespoons brown sugar
- 2 teaspoons dry mustard
- Salt and pepper to taste
- 1 tablespoon low-sodium Worcestershire sauce
- 1 cup cheddar cheese, shredded

Instructions:

1. Preheat your oven to 400 degrees F.

2. Prepare your pasta according to the directions in the packaging.

3. Drain and set aside.

4. Pour the oil in a pan over medium high heat.

5. Cook the turkey for 4 to 5 minutes, stirring frequently.

6. Stir in the garlic, onion, bell pepper and cauliflower rice.

7. Cook for 5 minutes.

8. Pour in the tomato sauce.

9. Stir in the sugar and mustard.

10. Season with the salt, pepper and Worcestershire sauce.

11. Bring to a boil.

12. Reduce heat and simmer for 2 minutes.

13. Add the pasta to the turkey mixture.

14. Spread the cheese on top.

15. Bake for 5 minutes.

Nutrients per Serving:

- Calories 481
- Fat 16.3 g
- Saturated fat 5.4 g
- Carbohydrates 57.6 g
- Fiber 9.3 g
- Protein 30 g
- Cholesterol 62 mg
- Sugars 12 g
- Sodium 639 mg
- Potassium 761 mg

Beef Enchilada Casserole

Add extra zing to this delicious beef casserole by pouring more hot sauce and chopped chili peppers into the mix. Otherwise, the recipe is good as it is, and is also very convenient to prepare.

Serving Size: 4

Preparation Cooking Time: 40 minutes

Ingredients:

Sauce

- 4 tablespoons butter
- ¼ cup all-purpose flour
- 3 cups low-fat milk
- ¼ cup Parmesan cheese, grated
- 2 ½ cups cheddar cheese, shredded
- Salt to taste

Enchiladas

- 2 teaspoons avocado oil
- 1 onion, diced
- 1 red bell pepper, diced
- 8 oz. lean ground beef
- 1 cup corn kernels
- 1 teaspoon garlic powder
- 2 teaspoons chili powder
- 1 tablespoon ground cumin
- 4 oz. canned diced green chili
- 8 corn tortillas, sliced into wedges
- 1 tomato, sliced and chopped

Instructions:

1. Prepare the cheese sauce by melting butter in a pan over medium heat.

2. Stir in the flour stir while cooking for 2 minutes.

3. Gradually add the milk and stir continuously for 10 minutes.

4. Remove from heat.

5. Add the Parmesan cheese and cheddar.

6. Season with the salt.

7. Preheat your oven to 400 degrees F.

8. Spray your baking pan with oil.

9. Pour the avocado oil in the pan over medium heat.

10. Next prepare the enchiladas.

11. Cook the onion, bell pepper and beef for 8 minutes.

12. Add the corn kernels.

13. Season with the garlic powder, chili powder and ground cumin.

14. Cook for 1 minute.

15. Turn off the heat.

16. Add the green chili and cheese sauce.

17. Arrange 1/3 of the tortillas in the baking pan.

18. Top with the beef mixture and half of the cheese sauce.

19. Repeat layers until ingredients have been used.

20. Bake in the oven for 15 minutes.

Nutrients per Serving:

- Calories 727
- Fat 45.7 g
- Saturated fat 13.7 g
- Carbohydrates 54.4 g
- Fiber 10.3 g
- Protein 26.4 g
- Cholesterol 77 mg
- Sugars 14 g
- Sodium 633 mg
- Potassium 759 mg

Eggplant Parmesan Casserole

If you love eggplant Parmesan, for sure, you're going to love this casserole version even more. Not only it has the same delicious flavors and creamy texture you love, it is also so much easier to make. On top of these, it's also lighter and healthier.

Serving Size: 8

Preparation Cooking Time: 1 hour and 10 minutes

Ingredients:

- 2 eggplants, sliced into rounds
- Salt and pepper to taste
- 2 tablespoons olive oil
- 1 cup onion, chopped
- 2 cloves garlic, crushed and minced
- ¼ cup dry red wine
- 28 oz. unsalted crushed tomatoes
- 1 teaspoon dried basil
- 1 teaspoon dried oregano
- 1 ½ cups mozzarella cheese, shredded
- ½ cup Parmesan cheese, grated
- Fresh basil, sliced

Instructions:

1. Preheat your oven to 400 degrees F.

2. Spray your baking pan with oil.

3. Spread the eggplant rounds on the baking pans.

4. Sprinkle with the salt and pepper.

5. Roast in the oven for 20 minutes.

6. Pour the oil into a pan over medium heat.

7. Cook the onion for 4 minutes.

8. Add the garlic and cook for 1 minute.

9. Stir in the wine, tomatoes, oregano and basil.

10. Season with the salt and pepper.

11. Simmer and then reduce heat.

12. Cook for 10 more minutes.

13. Spread 1 cup of this mixture in the baking pan.

14. Top with the eggplant rounds and then half of the cheeses.

15. Repeat the layers

16. Bake in the oven for 25 minutes.

17. Garnish with the chopped basil leaves and serve.

Nutrients per Serving:

- Calories 192
- Fat 9.3 g
- Saturated fat 3.7 g
- Carbohydrates 15.9 g
- Fiber 5.2 g
- Protein 9.5 g
- Cholesterol 18 mg
- Sugars 8 g
- Sodium 453 mg
- Potassium 632 mg

Tex-Mex Casserole

You're going to love the fusion of flavors in this Tex-Mex inspired casserole dish that comes together within only a few minutes of active preparations.

Serving Size: 6

Preparation Cooking Time: 3 hours and 30 minutes

Ingredients:

- 4 teaspoons olive oil
- 1 cup yellow onion, chopped
- 3 cloves garlic, crushed and minced
- 1 cup ground beef
- Salt to taste
- 1 teaspoon ground cumin
- 2 teaspoons chili powder
- 3 tomatoes, chopped
- ¼ cup fresh cilantro leaves, chopped
- 1 ½ cups corn kernels
- 2 teaspoons freshly squeezed lime juice
- Cooking spray
- 2 cups salsa
- 9 corn tortillas
- 1 ½ cups Mexican cheese blend, shredded

Instructions:

1. Pour 2 teaspoons oil in a pan over medium heat.

2. Cook the onions for 3 minutes.

3. Add the garlic and ground beef.

4. Cook for 4 minutes.

5. Season with the salt, cumin and chili powder.

6. Add half of the tomatoes.

7. In a bowl, mix the cilantro, corn and lime juice.

8. Stir in the remaining oil.

9. Spray your slow cooker with oil.

10. Spread half of the salsa in the pot.

11. Top with 3 tortillas.

12. Layer with the beef mixture, half of the salsa and half of the cheese.

13. Repeat the layers.

14. Cover the pot, then cook on low for 3 hours.

15. Top with the remaining tomatoes and cilantro mixture.

Nutrients per Serving:

- Calories 293
- Fat 13 g
- Saturated fat 5 g
- Carbohydrates 35 g
- Fiber 6 g
- Protein 17 g
- Cholesterol 13 mg
- Sugars 8 g
- Sodium 567 mg
- Potassium 254 mg

Cheesy Broccoli Rice Casserole

Turn an ordinary weeknight into something memorable for the whole family with this amazing cheesy broccoli and rice casserole. It has everything you're looking for in a casserole—tasty, healthy and best of all, easy to prepare!

Serving Size: 8

Preparation Cooking Time: 30 minutes

Ingredients:

- 1 tablespoon butter
- 1 cup onion, chopped
- 8 oz. mushrooms, chopped
- 1 tablespoon fresh thyme leaves, chopped
- 4 cloves garlic, crushed and minced
- 3 ½ cooked brown rice
- 2 tablespoons light mayonnaise
- ½ cup sour cream
- 1 teaspoon Dijon mustard
- 1 cup chicken broth (unsalted)
- Salt and pepper to taste
- 3 tablespoons cornstarch
- 3 cups broccoli florets, chopped
- 1 cup cheddar cheese, shredded

Instructions:

1. Preheat your broiler.

2. In pan over medium heat, add the butter and let it melt.

3. Cook the onion and mushrooms in butter for 7 minutes.

4. Stir in the thyme and garlic. Cook for 1 minute.

5. Add the rice, then stir to coat evenly and avoid clumping.

6. In a bowl, mix the mayo, sour cream, mustard, broth, salt and pepper.

7. Slowly add the cornstarch.

8. Mix well.

9. Pour the mixture into the pan.

10. Add the broccoli.

11. Stir to coat evenly.

12. Bring to a boil.

13. Cover and simmer for 7 minutes.

14. Sprinkle the top with cheese.

15. Broil for 2 minutes.

Nutrients per Serving:

- Calories 264
- Fat 12.1 g
- Saturated fat 5.4 g
- Carbohydrates 31.7 g
- Fiber 2.7 g
- Protein 8.2 g
- Cholesterol 26 mg
- Sugars 3 g
- Sodium 301 mg
- Potassium 373 mg

Squash Casserole

You can't go wrong with this simple appetizing squash casserole yet. It's creamy, cheesy and loaded with flavors you'll enjoy. Plus, it's full of essential nutrients. The trick is to drain all the water after boiling so the casserole doesn't end up soupy.

Serving Size: 6

Preparation Cooking Time: 45 minutes

Ingredients:

- Cooking spray
- 1 cup sweet onion, chopped
- 1 cup red bell pepper, chopped
- 1 cup chili pepper, chopped
- 6 cups summer squash, sliced
- ⅓ cup mayonnaise
- Salt and pepper to taste
- ⅔ cup cheddar cheese, shredded
- ⅔ cup breadcrumbs
- 1 tablespoon olive oil

Instructions:

1. Preheat your oven to 375 degrees F.

2. Spray your baking pan with oil.

3. Fill a pot with water.

4. Bring to a boil.

5. Add the onion, bell pepper, chili pepper and squash.

6. Cook for 6 minutes.

7. Drain and transfer to a plate.

8. Dry with paper towels.

9. In a bowl, mix the mayo, salt, pepper and cheese.

10. Add the squash mixture and toss to coat evenly.

11. Spread the mixture into the baking pan.

12. In a bowl, mix the oil and breadcrumbs.

13. Sprinkle on top of the squash.

14. Bake in the oven for 25 minutes.

15. Let cool for 5 minutes before serving.

Nutrients per Serving:

- Calories 235
- Fat 17 g
- Saturated fat 4 g
- Carbohydrates 17 g
- Fiber 4 g
- Protein 7 g
- Cholesterol 12 mg
- Sugars 6 g
- Sodium 301 mg
- Potassium 556 mg

Zucchini Casserole

There's so much to love about this zucchini casserole. Infused with Italian flavors, this is also one healthy dish loaded with tomatoes, basil, zucchini and mozzarella. Serve with couscous, quinoa or brown rice.

Serving Size: 6

Preparation Cooking Time: 1 hour

Ingredients:

- 2 zucchini, sliced
- 2 tomatoes, sliced
- 1 tablespoon olive oil
- ¼ cup shallot, chopped
- ¼ cup fresh basil leaves, chopped
- Salt and pepper to taste
- 3 oz. mozzarella cheese, shredded

Instructions:

1. Preheat your oven to 400 degrees F.

2. Spray your baking pan with oil.

3. Arrange the tomatoes and squash in the baking pan.

4. Mix the oil, shallot, basil, salt and pepper in a bowl.

5. Spread the mixture on top of the vegetables and sprinkle with mozzarella.

6. Bake in the oven for 30 minutes.

Nutrients per Serving:

- Calories 87
- Fat 5.4 g
- Saturated fat 2 g
- Carbohydrates 5.7 g
- Fiber 1.2 g
- Protein 4.8 g
- Cholesterol 9 mg
- Sugars 3 g
- Sodium 296 mg
- Potassium 326 mg

Baked Chicken Spaghetti Squash

If you love chicken and broccoli casserole, for sure, you're also going to enjoy this version. Instead of just broccoli, we also use spaghetti squash to make the dish creamier. And then we bake the casserole in mushroom soup.

Serving Size: 8

Preparation Cooking Time: 1 hour and 40 minutes

Ingredients:

- 3 lb. spaghetti squash
- 4 cups broccoli florets, steamed
- 1 tablespoon vegetable oil
- 1 onion, chopped
- ½ teaspoon dried thyme
- Pepper to taste
- 2 cloves garlic, crushed and minced
- 10 oz. mushrooms, sliced
- 20 oz. low sodium cream of mushroom soup
- 1 ½ lb. chicken breast fillet, chopped
- ½ cup cheddar cheese, shredded

Instructions:

1. Preheat your oven to 375 degrees F.

2. Spray your baking pan with oil.

3. Slice the squash lengthwise, then remove the seeds.

4. Microwave on high for 12 minutes.

5. Scrape the flesh and transfer to a plate. Set aside.

6. Pour the oil in a pan over medium heat.

7. Cook the mushrooms for 8 minutes.

8. Add the onion and cook for another 8 minutes.

9. Add the thyme, pepper and garlic. Cook for 30 seconds, stirring.

10. Stir in the squash, broccoli, and chicken.

11. Pour the mixture into the baking pan.

12. Top with the cheddar.

13. Cover with foil.

14. Bake in the oven for 25 minutes.

15. Remove the foil. Bake for another 10 minutes.

16. Let cool before serving.

Nutrients per Serving:

- Calories 273
- Fat 11.5 g
- Saturated fat 2.6 g
- Carbohydrates 18.5 g
- Fiber 4.6 g
- Protein 25.4 g
- Cholesterol 71 mg
- Sugars 6 g
- Sodium 493 mg
- Potassium 779 mg

Eggplant Casserole

Here's another eggplant casserole that you'd absolutely love. While the previous one is Italian-inspired, this one is infused with Tex-Mex flavors.

Serving Size: 8

Preparation Cooking Time: 1 hour and 10 minutes

Ingredients:

- 1 lb. eggplant, sliced into rounds
- 2 tablespoons vegetable oil, divided
- 2 onions, sliced thinly
- 3 cloves garlic, crushed and minced
- 1 teaspoon ground cumin
- 2 teaspoons dried oregano
- 1 teaspoon onion powder
- 1 tablespoon chili powder
- 30 oz. unsalted black beans, rinsed and drained
- ¼ cup fresh cilantro leaves, chopped
- 9 oz. canned mild green chili
- 28 oz. canned diced tomatoes
- 10 corn tortillas, quartered
- 1 cup cheddar cheese, shredded

Instructions:

1. Preheat your oven to 375 degrees F.

2. Spray your baking pan with oil.

3. Arrange the eggplant rounds in a baking pan.

4. Brush with half of the oil.

5. Bake in the oven for 15 minutes.

6. Pour the remaining oil in a pan over medium heat.

7. Cook the onion for 10 minutes.

8. Add the garlic and season with the spices. Cook for 30 seconds.

9. Add the beans, cilantro, chili and tomatoes.

10. Remove from heat and set aside.

11. Then arrange half of the tortillas in the baking pan

12. Top with half of the tomatoes and beans, and then with half of the eggplant and half of the cheese.

13. Repeat the layers.

14. Cover with foil.

15. Bake in the oven for 30 minutes.

16. Remove the foil. Bake for another 10 minutes.

Nutrients per Serving:

- Calories 304
- Fat 10.1 g
- Saturated fat 3 g
- Carbohydrates 41.3 g
- Fiber 10.2 g
- Protein 14.2 g
- Cholesterol 13 mg
- Sugars 8 g
- Sodium 250 mg
- Potassium 488 mg

Breakfast Casserole

Start the day with a delicious surprise with this sausage and mushrooms casserole that everyone will surely be delighted with.

Serving Size: 6

Preparation Cooking Time: 3 hours and 30 minutes

Ingredients:

- 2 teaspoons olive oil
- 1 cup button mushrooms, sliced
- 1 red sweet pepper, chopped
- 1 onion, chopped
- 8 oz. baguette bread, sliced into cubes
- 6 oz. smoked turkey sausage, sliced thinly
- ½ cup Swiss cheese, shredded
- 4 eggs
- 3 egg whites
- 1 teaspoon dried oregano, crushed
- 2 cups nonfat milk

Instructions:

1. In pan over medium heat, add the oil and cook the onion, mushrooms and sweet pepper for 5 minutes.

2. Spray your baking pan with oil.

3. Then arrange half of the bread slices in the pan.

4. Top with half of the mushrooms, half of the sausage and half of the cheese.

5. Repeat the layers.

6. In a bowl, beat eggs and egg whites.

7. Stir in the oregano and milk.

8. Pour this mixture on top of the casserole.

9. Preheat your oven to 350 degrees F.

10. Bake in the oven for 50 minutes.

11. Let it cool around 10 minutes before slicing and serving.

Nutrients per Serving:

- Calories 285
- Fat 11.5 g
- Saturated fat 3.2 g
- Carbohydrates 25 g
- Fiber 5.2 g
- Protein 21.8 g
- Cholesterol 168 mg
- Sugars 9 g
- Sodium 533 mg
- Potassium 834 mg

Oatmeal Casserole

When you think of casserole, you immediately imagine meat, veggies and cheese. Now here's a different kind of casserole that's made with oatmeal, but will fascinate and satisfy you nonetheless.

Serving Size: 2

Preparation Cooking Time: 30 minutes

Ingredients:

- Cooking spray
- 1 cup nonfat milk
- 2 teaspoons butter
- ½ cup rolled oats
- 1 apple, chopped
- 3 tablespoons raisins
- 2 tablespoons walnuts, toasted and chopped
- ¼ teaspoon vanilla extract
- Salt to taste
- 2 teaspoons brown sugar

Instructions:

1. Spray your casserole with oil.

2. In a pan over medium heat, boil the butter and milk.

3. Add the oats and the rest of the ingredients.

4. Cook while stirring for 2 minutes.

5. Transfer to the casserole.

6. Bake in your oven at 350 degrees F for 10 to 12 minutes.

Nutrients per Serving:

- Calories 299
- Fat 9.8 g
- Saturated fat 1.5 g
- Carbohydrates 44.8 g
- Fiber 5.3 g
- Protein 9.7 g
- Cholesterol 2 mg
- Sugars 24 g
- Sodium 248 mg
- Potassium 387 mg

Shrimp Casserole

This is another delicious Mexican-inspired casserole wherein the shrimp takes center stage. You're going to love how the flavors from the different ingredients blend together to create a truly unforgettable dish.

Serving Size: 6

Preparation Cooking Time: an hour and 30 minutes

Ingredients:

- 6 corn tortillas, sliced into strips
- ½ cup light sour cream
- 1 cup green salsa
- 3 tablespoons all-purpose flour
- 4 oz. grated Monterey Jack cheese
- 4 tablespoons fresh cilantro, chopped and divided
- 12 oz. shrimp, cooked, peeled and deveined
- 1 tomato, chopped
- 1 cup corn kernels

Instructions:

1. Preheat your oven to 350 degrees F.

2. Arrange half of the tortilla strips in a baking dish.

3. In a bowl, mix the sour cream, salsa, flour, cheese and cilantro.

4. In another bowl, mix the shrimp, tomatoes and corn kernels.

5. Top the tortillas with the sour cream mixture, and then with the shrimp mixture.

6. Repeat layers.

7. Bake in the oven for 40 minutes.

Nutrients per Serving:

- Calories 242
- Fat 7.7 g
- Saturated fat 3.7 g
- Carbohydrates 25.4 g
- Fiber 3.4 g
- Protein 20.2 g
- Cholesterol 129 mg
- Sugars 3 g
- Sodium 564 mg
- Potassium 340 mg

Turkey Broccoli Casserole

In this recipe, we combine turkey fillet and broccoli florets, and turned it into a cheesy and creamy casserole that you can serve when your friends come over for a visit.

Serving Size: 8

Preparation Cooking Time: 40 minutes

Ingredients:

- 1 tablespoon vegetable oil
- 1 lb. chicken breast fillet, trimmed
- 4 cups low-fat milk, divided
- ¼ cup all-purpose flour
- 3 cups broccoli florets
- 4 cups cooked brown rice
- 2 cups low-fat cheddar cheese, shredded
- Salt and pepper to taste
- Crispy fried onions

Instructions:

1. Preheat your oven to 400 degrees F.

2. Pour the oil in a pan over medium high heat.

3. Cook the chicken for 5 minutes per side.

4. Transfer to a cutting board. Slice into cubes.

5. In a bowl, combine half of the milk and flour.

6. Add the remaining milk to the pan.

7. Bring to a boil.

8. Slowly add the flour and milk mixture.

9. Keep boiling while stirring for 2 minutes.

10. Add the broccoli and rice.

11. Cook for 2 minutes.

12. Stir in the cheese and chicken.

13. Season with the salt and pepper.

14. Add the onions on top.

15. Transfer the skillet to the oven.

16. Bake for 10 minutes.

17. Let cool before serving.

Nutrients per Serving:

- Calories 353
- Fat 13.1 g
- Saturated fat 5.1 g
- Carbohydrates 30.8 g
- Fiber 1.7 g
- Protein 24.6 g
- Cholesterol 56 mg
- Sugars 6 g
- Sodium 413 mg
- Potassium 404 mg

Cauliflower Casserole

Once you get a taste of the amazing cauliflower casserole recipe, you might never want to prepare cauliflower differently ever again.

Serving Size: 8

Preparation Cooking Time: 1 hour

Ingredients:

- 3 slices bacon
- 2 lb. cauliflower florets
- Salt and pepper to taste
- ⅔ cup sour cream
- 1 ¼ cups cheddar cheese, shredded
- 4 scallions, sliced

Instructions:

1. Preheat your oven to 425 degrees F.

2. Cook bacon in pan over medium heat for 8 minutes.

3. Drain on a plate lined with paper towel but reserve drippings.

4. Chop the bacon into smaller pieces.

5. Toss the cauliflower in the bacon drippings and season with the pepper and salt in a baking pan.

6. Bake in the oven for 35 minutes.

7. In a bowl, mix the sour cream, cheddar and scallions.

8. Top the cauliflower with this mixture.

9. Sprinkle the crumbled bacon on top.

10. Bake in the oven for 5 minutes.

Nutrients per Serving:

- Calories 150
- Fat 10.5 g
- Saturated fat 5.5 g
- Carbohydrates 7.6 g
- Fiber 2.5 g
- Protein 7.9 g
- Cholesterol 30 mg
- Sugars 3 g
- Sodium 280 mg
- Potassium 412 mg

Green Bean Casserole

Looking for a light casserole that won't give you too many calories? Try this green casserole. It's the casserole version of your favorite green bean salad.

Serving Size: 8

Preparation Cooking Time: 40 minutes

Ingredients:

- 3 tablespoons olive oil, divided
- ½ cup shallots, sliced thinly
- 8 oz. mushrooms, sliced
- 1 lb. green beans, trimmed and sliced in half
- ¼ cup water
- 3 cloves garlic, crushed and minced
- 1 tablespoon white-wine vinegar
- 1 teaspoon dried thyme
- Salt and pepper to taste
- 1 tablespoon Dijon mustard
- 4 cups chard, chopped
- 3 cups sourdough bread, sliced into cubes and toasted

Instructions:

1. Pour 2 tablespoons oil in a pan over medium heat.

2. Cook the shallots for 4 minutes.

3. Transfer to plate lined with paper towel.

4. Add the remaining oil to the skillet. Cook the mushrooms for 6 minutes.

5. Transfer to another plate.

6. Cook the green beans in water for 5 minutes.

7. In a bowl, mix the garlic, vinegar, thyme, salt, pepper and mustard.

8. Add this mixture to the beans. Cook for 30 seconds.

9. Add the mushrooms, chard and toasted bread on top.

Nutrients per Serving:

- Calories 116
- Fat 5.6 g
- Saturated fat 0.8 g
- Carbohydrates 14.5 g
- Fiber 2.4 g
- Protein 3.8 g
- Cholesterol 10 mg
- Sugars 3 g
- Sodium 299 mg
- Potassium 355 mg

Herbed Garlic Potato Casserole

The secret to this recipe is roasting the garlic before adding it to the mix. It gives the casserole not only an appetizing aroma but a strong flavor that you won't get enough of.

Serving Size: 8

Preparation Cooking Time: 1 hour and 20 minutes

Ingredients:

- 2 lb. potatoes, sliced into wedges
- 3 tablespoons olive oil
- 1 teaspoon herb and garlic seasoning
- Pepper to taste
- 1 bulb garlic
- Salt to taste
- 1 cup Greek yogurt
- ¼ cup Parmesan cheese, grated
- ¼ cup parsley, snipped

Instructions:

1. Preheat your oven to 325 degrees F.

2. Add the potatoes to a baking pan.

3. Toss in 1 tablespoon oil.

4. Season with the herb and garlic mix.

5. Toss to coat evenly.

6. Slice the top off the garlic.

7. Drizzle the garlic with the remaining oil.

8. Add the garlic to the pan.

9. Roast for 50 minutes.

10. Squeeze the garlic into the potatoes.

11. Mash the potatoes.

12. Spread it with the yogurt.

13. Sprinkle the cheese and chopped parsley on top before serving.

Nutrients per Serving:

- Calories 157
- Fat 6 g
- Saturated fat 1.1 g
- Carbohydrates 20.9 g
- Fiber 2.1 g
- Protein 6 g
- Cholesterol 3 mg
- Sugars 3 g
- Sodium 148 mg
- Potassium 552 mg

Ham Egg Casserole

This is one ham and egg casserole with a special twist you're going to love—it's made with apples. The apples do a great job in balancing the flavors, and of course, adding more nutrients to the dish.

Serving Size: 8

Preparation Cooking Time: an hour and 30 minutes

Ingredients:

- 6 oz. rye bread, sliced into cubes
- 6 oz. reduced-sodium ham, chopped
- 1 cup apple, chopped
- 4 oz. cheddar cheese, shredded
- 2 cups nonfat milk
- 6 eggs, beaten
- Pepper to taste
- ½ cup green onions, sliced thinly

Instructions:

1. Preheat your oven to 325 degrees F.

2. Spray your baking pan with oil.

3. Then arrange half of the bread cubes in the baking pan.

4. Top with the apples, ham and cheese.

5. Sprinkle the remaining bread on top.

6. In a bowl, beat eggs and stir in the milk and pepper.

7. Sprinkle the green onions on top.

8. Bake in the oven for 50 minutes.

9. Let cool for 10 minutes before serving.

Nutrients per Serving:

- Calories 180
- Fat 4 g
- Saturated fat 2.2 g
- Carbohydrates 19.5 g
- Fiber 2.1 g
- Protein 16.3 g
- Cholesterol 20 mg
- Sugars 8 g
- Sodium 522 mg
- Potassium 318 mg

Zucchini Pizza Casserole

Want to enjoy pizza without the guilt? Make this light and healthy pizza casserole with zucchini. It's topped with your favorite ingredients, bell pepper, pepperoni, and cheese.

Serving Size: 6

Preparation Cooking Time: 1 hour

Ingredients:

- 2 zucchini, shredded
- ¼ cup onion, chopped
- 2 tablespoons all-purpose flour
- 4 eggs, beaten
- ¼ cup Parmesan cheese, grated
- 1 clove garlic, minced
- ¼ cup fresh basil leaves, chopped
- 1 cup canned tomatoes, crushed
- Salt and pepper to taste
- 1 cup mozzarella cheese, shredded
- ¼ cup pepperoni
- 2 green bell peppers, sliced thinly

Instructions:

1. Preheat your oven to 400 degrees F.

2. Spray your baking pan with oil.

3. Squeeze the zucchini with paper towel to remove excess water.

4. Place in a bowl.

5. Combine with the onions, flour, eggs and cheese.

6. Spread the mixture in the baking pan.

7. Bake for 30 minutes.

8. In a bowl, mix the garlic, basil and tomatoes.

9. Season with the salt and pepper.

10. Spread this sauce on top of the zucchini crust.

11. Sprinkle the cheese, pepperoni and bell pepper on top.

12. Bake in the oven for another 15 minutes.

Nutrients per Serving:

- Calories 190
- Fat 10.4 g
- Saturated fat 4.6 g
- Carbohydrates 11 g
- Fiber 2.2 g
- Protein 13.1 g
- Cholesterol 144 mg
- Sugars 5 g
- Sodium 414 mg
- Potassium 550 mg

Turkey Zucchini Lasagna

There are now many ways to make lasagna. For sure, once you've tried preparing this particular recipe, you're going to prepare lasagna using this method more often. It's not only delicious and creamy, it's also super healthy.

Serving Size: 6

Preparation Cooking Time: 3 hours

Ingredients:

- 1 tablespoon olive oil
- 1 onion, chopped
- 6 cloves garlic, minced
- 1 carrot, shredded
- 1 teaspoon dried oregano
- 3 tablespoons tomato paste
- 28 oz. canned crushed tomatoes
- 6 cups turkey fillet, cooked and shredded
- ½ teaspoon red pepper flakes
- 1 cup nonfat cottage cheese
- Pinch ground nutmeg
- 1 egg white
- 2 tablespoons fresh basil leaves, snipped
- 1 oz. mozzarella cheese, shredded
- Cooking spray
- 3 zucchinis, sliced, boiled and dried

Instructions:

1. In pan over medium heat, cook the onion, garlic, carrot and oregano for 5 minutes.

2. Add the tomatoes paste and tomatoes.

3. Bring to boil and then simmer for 10 minutes. Set aside.

4. Add the cottage cheese, nutmeg and egg white to a blender.

5. Pulse until smooth.

6. Stir in the basil and half of the mozzarella cheese. Set aside.

7. Spray your baking pan with oil.

8. Then arrange half of the zucchini slices on the bottom of the pan.

9. Top with half of the tomato mixture and half of the cottage cheese mixture.

10. Repeat the layers.

11. Then bake in the oven at 350 degrees F for 1 hour and 30 minutes.

12. Sprinkle the remaining mozzarella cheese on top.

13. Bake lastly for another 5 minutes or until the cheese has melted.

Nutrients per Serving:

- Calories 293
- Fat 12.1 g
- Saturated fat 3.7 g
- Carbohydrates 20.9 g
- Fiber 5.1 g
- Protein 24.9 g
- Cholesterol 66 mg
- Sugars 12 g
- Sodium 346 mg
- Potassium 1209 mg

Apple Sweet Potato Casserole

You can expect healthy goodness from this casserole dish, thanks to the combination of apples and sweet potatoes. Making the dish a little more interesting is the sprinkling of bacon on top. Use turkey bacon if you want something lighter.

Serving Size: 6

Preparation Cooking Time: 1 hour

Ingredients:

- Cooking spray
- 2 cups apples, chopped
- ½ cup onion, chopped
- 10 oz. sweet potatoes, sliced into cubes
- Pepper to taste
- 2 teaspoons fresh thyme leaves, snipped
- 6 eggs, beaten
- ¾ cup fat-free milk
- 3 oz. low-fat cheddar cheese, shredded
- 10 slices bacon, cooked crispy and chopped

Instructions:

1. Preheat your oven to 350 degrees F.

2. Spray your muffin cups with oil.

3. Add the onion and apples in a pan over medium heat. Cook for 5 minutes.

4. Stir in the sweet potatoes and cook for another 10 minutes.

5. Season with the pepper and thyme.

6. Add the potato mixture into the muffin cups.

7. In a bowl, mix the milk and egg.

8. Pour this mixture over the potatoes.

9. Top with the cheese.

10. Bake in the oven for 30 minutes.

11. Sprinkle the top with bacon before serving.

Nutrients per Serving:

- Calories 198
- Fat 6 g
- Saturated fat 3 g
- Carbohydrates 22 g
- Fiber 3 g
- Protein 15 g
- Cholesterol 16 mg
- Sugars 11 g
- Sodium 387 mg
- Potassium 556 mg

Cheesy Zucchini Frittata

A simple but delicious casserole that you can get done within only a few minutes—serve this for breakfast, lunch or dinner.

Serving Size: 4

Preparation Cooking Time: 30 minutes

Ingredients:

- 4 eggs, beaten
- ½ cup low-fat cheddar cheese
- 2 tablespoons parsley, snipped
- Salt and pepper to taste
- 4 green onions, chopped
- 12 oz. zucchini, sliced

Instructions:

1. Preheat your oven to 450 degrees F.

2. In a bowl, mix the eggs, cheese and parsley.

3. Season with the salt and pepper.

4. Pour the oil into a pan over medium high heat.

5. Cook the green onion and zucchini for 5 minutes.

6. Pour the egg mixture on top of zucchini.

7. Reduce heat and simmer until eggs are cooked on the edges.

8. Place in your oven and bake for 5 minutes.

Nutrients per Serving:

- Calories 115
- Fat 5.5 g
- Saturated fat 2.4 g
- Carbohydrates 5.7 g
- Fiber 1.4 g
- Protein 10.9 g
- Cholesterol 10 mg
- Sugars 2 g
- Sodium 321 mg
- Potassium 385 mg

Cheese Mushroom Casserole

Cheese and mushroom have always been a popular combination when it comes to dishes. In this casserole recipe, we also include grits, eggs and some spices to make this dish even more palatable.

Serving Size: 6

Preparation Cooking Time: 1 hour

Ingredients:

- Cooking spray
- 3 cups water
- 1 cup grits
- ¾ cup cheddar cheese, shredded
- Salt to taste
- 8 oz. button mushrooms, sliced
- 6 oz. Portobello mushrooms, sliced
- Pepper to taste
- 4 oz. prosciutto, chopped
- 2 cloves garlic, minced
- 5 eggs, beaten

Instructions:

1. Preheat your oven to 350 degrees F.

2. Spray your baking pan with oil.

3. Fill a small pot with water. Bring to a boil.

4. Cook the grits for 6 to 7 minutes.

5. Remove from heat.

6. Add ¼ cup of cheese and season with salt.

7. Spread this mixture in the baking pan.

8. Spray your pan with oil.

9. Place it over medium heat. (Do not spray oil when the stove is already working).

10. Cook the mushrooms for 5 minutes.

11. Season with the pepper.

12. Add the garlic and prosciutto. Cook for 1 minute.

13. Stir in the eggs to the mixture.

14. Add this to the baking pan.

15. Sprinkle the top with the remaining cheese.

16. Bake for 30 minutes.

Nutrients per Serving:

- Calories 235
- Fat 10 g
- Saturated fat 2 g
- Carbohydrates 23 g
- Fiber 2 g
- Protein 17 g
- Cholesterol 81 mg
- Sugars 2 g
- Sodium 571 mg
- Potassium 335 mg

Polenta Lasagna

Polenta refers to a popular Northern Italian cornmeal mush that is usually served in lieu of pasta. Use this as the base for this vegetarian lasagna.

Serving Size: 8

Preparation Cooking Time: 2 hours and 20 minutes

Ingredients:

- 4 cups cold water, divided
- 1 ½ cups cornmeal
- Salt to taste
- 1 tablespoon olive oil
- 1 onion, sliced thinly
- 4 cups mushrooms, sliced in half
- Pepper to taste
- 3 red bell peppers, roasted and sliced into small pieces
- 3 green bell peppers, roasted and sliced into small pieces
- 1 ¼ cups marinara sauce
- 4 oz. mozzarella cheese, shredded

Instructions:

1. Pour 2 ½ cups of water in your small pot.

2. Bring to a boil.

3. In a bowl, add the remaining water, cornmeal and salt.

4. Add gradually the cornmeal mixture to the boiling water.

5. Bring to a boil.

6. Reduce heat and simmer for 10 minutes.

7. Let cool and then transfer to a baking pan.

8. Preheat your oven to 350 degrees F.

9. Pour the oil into a pan over medium heat.

10. Cook the onion for 3 minutes.

11. Add the mushrooms and season with the salt and pepper.

12. Cook for 5 minutes.

13. Remove from the stove.

14. Add the bell peppers.

15. Spread thin layer of the marinara sauce on top of the polenta.

16. Top with the mushrooms and cheese.

17. Bake in the oven for 30 minutes.

Nutrients per Serving:

- Calories 188
- Fat 6.7 g
- Saturated fat 2.3 g
- Carbohydrates 27.2 g
- Fiber 4.2 g
- Protein 7.6 g
- Cholesterol 8 mg
- Sugars 3 g
- Sodium 649 mg
- Potassium 473 mg

Green Bean Casserole

You don't have to wait for the special occasion to serve this awesome casserole dish. It's ready in just a few minutes.

Serving Size: 10

Preparation Cooking Time: 30 minutes

Ingredients:

- ½ cup nonfat milk
- 4 oz. low-fat cream cheese
- 2 cloves garlic, minced
- Pepper to taste
- 2 lb. green beans steamed
- ½ cup light sour cream
- Cooked onion rings

Instructions:

1. In a pan over medium low heat, add the milk, cream cheese, garlic and pepper.

2. Cook while stirring for 2 minutes.

3. Stir in the green beans and sour cream.

4. Spread the mixture in a baking pan.

5. Bake in the oven at 350 degrees F for 15 minutes.

6. Top with crispy onion rings.

Nutrients per Serving:

- Calories 88
- Fat 3.9 g
- Saturated fat 2.3 g
- Carbohydrates 10.4 g
- Fiber 3 g
- Protein 4.2 g
- Cholesterol 12 mg
- Sugars 3 g
- Sodium 79 mg
- Potassium 232 mg

Potato Sausage Casserole

There's nothing more you can ask for from this ultimate casserole dish—it's full of flavor, nutrients, and you'll love that it's a cinch to prepare.

Serving Size: 12

Preparation Cooking Time: 1 hour

Ingredients:

- Cooking spray
- ½ cup onion, chopped
- 1 sweet red pepper, sliced into strips
- 8 oz. Italian turkey sausage
- 3 cups hash brown potatoes, diced
- Pepper to taste
- 1 teaspoon dried oregano, crushed
- ½ cup feta cheese, crumbled
- ¾ cup nonfat milk
- 5 eggs, beaten

Instructions:

1. Preheat your oven to 350 degrees F.

2. Spray your muffin cups with oil.

3. Spray your pan with oil and put it over medium heat.

4. Cook the onion, red pepper and sausage for 4 minutes.

5. Add the potatoes and season with the pepper and oregano.

6. Cook for 3 minutes.

7. Pour the sausage mixture into the muffin cups.

8. Mix the milk and eggs and pour on top of the sausages.

9. Sprinkle the cheese on top.

10. Bake for 25 minutes.

Nutrients per Serving:

- Calories 215
- Fat 10 g
- Saturated fat 3 g
- Carbohydrates 17 g
- Fiber 2 g
- Protein 16 g
- Cholesterol 183 mg
- Sugars 3 g
- Sodium 438 mg
- Potassium 556 mg

Mexican Beef Bake

This incredible casserole dish is made with pasta, ground beef and beans, and topped with sour cream and cheese. Expect it to be the huge hit when you serve it to friends and family.

Serving Size: 6

Preparation Cooking Time: 1 hour

Ingredients:

- 4 oz. elbow macaroni
- 12 oz. lean ground beef
- 2 cloves garlic, crushed and minced
- 15 oz. black beans, rinsed and drained
- 15 oz. unsalted diced tomatoes
- ¾ cup salsa
- 1 teaspoon dried oregano flakes
- ½ teaspoon chili powder
- ½ teaspoon ground cumin
- ¼ cup sour cream
- 2 teaspoons cilantro, chopped
- 3 tablespoons green onions, sliced
- ½ teaspoon lime zest
- 2 oz. Monterey Jack cheese, shredded

Instructions:

1. Preheat your oven to 350 degrees F.

2. Prepare your pasta according to the directions in the package.

3. Drain and set aside.

4. In a pan over medium heat, cook the garlic and beef for 5 minutes.

5. Drain the fat.

6. Transfer the beef to a baking pan.

7. Stir in the pasta and the rest of the ingredients except the cheese, sour cream and lime zest.

8. Bake in the oven for 30 minutes.

9. Top with the cheese and bake for another 3 minutes.

10. In a bowl, mix the sour cream and lime zest.

11. Top the pasta with this mixture and serve.

Nutrients per Serving:

- Calories 283
- Fat 9.6 g
- Saturated fat 4.1 g
- Carbohydrates 29.4 g
- Fiber 6.5 g
- Protein 22.6 g
- Cholesterol 45 mg
- Sugars 4 g
- Sodium 520 mg
- Potassium 469 mg

Chicken Cordon Bleu Casserole

Chicken cordon bleu is one of the world's most popular dishes. And now you can make it even more special (and easier to prepare) by turning it into a casserole dish.

Serving Size: 6

Preparation Cooking Time: 1 hour and 20 minutes

Ingredients:

- 2 cups broccoli florets, steamed and chopped
- 8 oz. whole-wheat fusilli, cooked
- 2 tablespoons butter
- 1 lb. chicken breast fillet, sliced into cubes
- 1 onion, chopped
- Salt and pepper to taste
- 3 tablespoons all-purpose flour
- 2 tablespoons Dijon mustard
- 2 cups low-fat milk
- 4 oz. diced cooked ham
- 1 cup Swiss cheese, shredded
- 1 tablespoon olive oil
- 1 cup breadcrumbs
- ½ cup parsley, chopped

Instructions:

1. Preheat your oven to 375 degrees F.

2. Melt the butter in pan over medium heat.

3. Cook the onion and chicken for 7 minutes.

4. Season with the salt and pepper.

5. Add the mustard and flour.

6. Mix well.

7. Pour in the milk and boil for 3 minutes.

8. Transfer to a bowl.

9. Add the pasta, broccoli, ham and cheese.

10. Spread the mixture in a baking pan.

11. Mix the oil and breadcrumbs.

12. Add this on top of the pasta mixture.

13. Sprinkle the parsley on top.

14. Bake in the oven for 30 minutes.

Nutrients per Serving:

- Calories 495
- Fat 16.9 g
- Saturated fat 7.4 g
- Carbohydrates 47.1 g
- Fiber 5.7 g
- Protein 37.7 g
- Cholesterol 87 mg
- Sugars 6 g
- Sodium 719 mg
- Potassium 471 mg

Salmon Casserole

Add couscous, bell pepper and spinach to this simple salmon casserole dish to make it extra special.

Serving Size: 4

Preparation Cooking Time: 30 minutes

Ingredients:

- 2 cloves garlic, minced
- 1 cup water
- ⅔ cup whole wheat couscous
- 15 oz. salmon flakes
- 2 cups baby spinach
- ½ cup roasted red sweet peppers, chopped
- ¼ cup tomato sauce
- 2 tablespoons almonds, toasted and chopped

Instructions:

1. Microwave the garlic and water on high for 3 minutes.

2. Stir in the couscous.

3. Transfer to a serving plate.

4. Spread the salmon on top of the couscous and cover with foil.

5. Let stand for 5 minutes.

6. Stir in the rest of the ingredients.

Nutrients per Serving:

- Calories 335
- Fat 9.3 g
- Saturated fat 2 g
- Carbohydrates 34.4 g
- Fiber 5.8 g
- Protein 29.7 g
- Cholesterol 41 mg
- Sugars 1 g
- Sodium 616 mg
- Potassium 464 mg

Turkey Rice Casserole

Sure to be a crowd pleaser, this turkey and rice casserole is made with lean turkey fillet, mushrooms, zucchini and brown rice topped with cheese and breadcrumbs.

Serving Size: 6

Preparation Cooking Time: 1 hour and 10 minutes

Ingredients:

- 1 cup uncooked brown rice
- 1 ½ cups water
- ⅓ cup cream cheese
- 1 egg, beaten
- ½ cup nonfat milk
- Salt to taste
- 1 teaspoon dried Italian seasoning, crushed
- 2 oz. Parmesan cheese, shredded
- 2 tablespoons olive oil
- ½ cup onion, chopped
- 4 cloves garlic, crushed and minced
- 2 cups button mushrooms, sliced in half
- 1 zucchini, sliced thinly
- 8 oz. turkey breast fillet, sliced into strips
- ½ cup breadcrumbs

Instructions:

1. In pan over medium heat, mix the rice and water.

2. Bring to a boil.

3. Reduce heat and simmer for 40 minutes.

4. Remove from heat.

5. Stir in the cream cheese.

6. Let sit for 5 minutes.

7. Stir in the egg, milk, salt, Italian seasoning and half of the Parmesan cheese.

8. Mix well.

9. Preheat your oven to 375 degrees F.

10. Pour 1 tablespoon oil into a pan over medium heat.

11. Cook the onion, garlic, mushrooms and zucchini for 7 minutes.

12. Add this to the rice.

13. Add the remaining oil to the pan.

14. Cook the turkey for 5 minutes.

15. Stir into the rice mixture.

16. Spread in a baking pan.

17. Top with the remaining cheese.

18. Bake for 20 minutes.

Nutrients per Serving:

- Calories 321
- Fat 12.9 g
- Saturated fat 4.3 g
- Carbohydrates 33.2 g
- Fiber 2.5 g
- Protein 19 g
- Cholesterol 67 mg
- Sugars 4 g
- Sodium 382 mg
- Potassium 488 mg

Tuna Casserole

Turn your tuna casserole into something extra special by adding feta cheese, artichoke hearts, olives, eggplant and oregano.

Serving Size: 6

Preparation Cooking Time: 1 hour and 15 minutes

Ingredients:

- 1 eggplant, sliced
- 1 red sweet pepper, sliced
- 1 clove garlic, crushed and minced
- 2 tablespoons lemon juice
- 1 ½ teaspoons lemon zest
- 2 tablespoons olive oil
- Salt and pepper to taste
- 4 tablespoons fresh oregano, snipped
- ¼ cup orzo pasta, prepared according to the package directions
- 9 oz. artichoke hearts, sliced into wedges
- ¼ cup feta cheese, crumbled
- ½ cup ripe olives, sliced in half
- 15 oz. canned tuna flakes
- ½ cup Panko breadcrumbs

Instructions:

1. Preheat your oven to 425 degrees F.

2. Spray your baking pan with oil.

3. Spray the eggplant slices with oil and add to the pan.

4. Toss in the sweet peppers.

5. Roast in the oven for 20 minutes.

6. In a bowl, mix the garlic, olive oil, lemon juice and lemon zest.

7. Season with the salt, pepper and oregano.

8. In another bowl, mix the orzo, sweet pepper, eggplant, artichoke hearts, feta cheese, olives, tuna flakes and breadcrumbs.

9. Add the lemon dressing and mix.

10. Pour the mixture into the pan.

11. Bake in your oven at 350 degrees F for 40 minutes.

Nutrients per Serving:

- Sugars 5 g
- Calories 239
- Fat 8.4 g
- Cholesterol 37 mg
- Saturated fat 1.8 g
- Carbohydrates 23.8 g
- Potassium 317 mg
- Fiber 9.1 g
- Protein 20.2 g
- Sodium 436 mg

Tuna Pasta Casserole

Here's another tuna casserole that's sure to captivate your taste buds—this one is made with broccoli, mushrooms, onions, and low-fat milk.

Serving Size: 4

Preparation Cooking Time: 1 hour

Ingredients:

- 1 cup onion, chopped
- 2 cups mushrooms, sliced
- 3 oz. noodles
- 1 cup stir-fry vegetables
- 1 cup broccoli florets
- ¾ cup low-fat milk
- 11 oz. low-fat mushroom soup
- Salt to taste
- 1/2 teaspoon dried dill
- 6 oz. tuna flakes
- 2 tablespoons Parmesan cheese, grated

Instructions:

1. Preheat your oven to 375 degrees F.

2. In pan over medium heat, cook the onion, mushrooms, noodles, stir-fry veggies and broccoli in hot water for 3 minutes.

3. Drain and set aside.

4. In a bowl, mix the milk, cream of mushroom, salt and dill.

5. Add to the noodles.

6. Stir in the tuna flakes.

7. Transfer the mixture to a baking pan.

8. Bake for 25 minutes.

9. Sprinkle the Parmesan cheese on top. Bake for another 5 minutes.

Nutrients per Serving:

- Calories 222
- Fat 4 g
- Saturated fat 1.4 g
- Carbohydrates 27.5 g
- Fiber 2.5 g
- Protein 18.2 g
- Cholesterol 45 mg
- Sugars 6 g
- Sodium 685 mg
- Potassium 596 mg

Baked Penne

Of all the baked penne dishes, this one will surely satisfy your cravings. But that's not all, it's also packed with protein and other essential nutrients.

Serving Size: 6

Preparation Cooking Time: 1 hour and 10 minutes

Ingredients:

- 2 cloves garlic, crushed and minced
- 10 oz. spinach, chopped
- ¼ cup vegetable broth
- 8 oz. whole penne pasta, cooked according to package directions
- ½ cup raw cashews
- 1 onion, chopped
- Salt and pepper to taste
- 2 teaspoons lemon juice
- ½ cup whole wheat breadcrumbs
- 1 ¾ cups water
- ½ teaspoon dry mustard
- 16 oz. white kidney beans, rinsed and drained

Instructions:

1. Preheat your oven to 375 degrees F.

2. Combine the cooked pasta and spinach in a baking pan.

3. In a pan over medium heat, boil the onion and garlic in the broth.

4. Reduce heat and simmer for 5 minutes.

5. Remove from the stove. Set aside.

6. Add the cashews to the processor. Pulse until finely ground.

7. Stir in the water.

8. Add the onion mixture, salt, bean, pepper, mustard and lemon juice

9. Add the bean mixture to the pasta.

10. Top with the breadcrumbs.

11. Bake in the oven for 30 minutes.

12. Serve immediately.

Nutrients per Serving:

- Calories 315
- Fat 7.7 g
- Saturated fat 1.3 g
- Carbohydrates 53.3 g
- Fiber 10.1 g
- Protein 14.5 g
- Cholesterol 12 mg
- Sugars 3 g
- Sodium 198 mg
- Potassium 564 mg

Cheesy Turkey Casserole

You'll be satisfied with every bite of this cheesy turkey casserole.

Serving Size: 6

Preparation Cooking Time: 1 hour and 10 minutes

Ingredients:

- 2 cups mushrooms, sliced
- ¾ cup red sweet pepper, chopped
- ½ cup onion, chopped
- 2 cloves garlic, crushed and minced
- 2 tablespoons butter
- ¼ cup all-purpose flour
- ½ teaspoon dried thyme
- Salt and pepper to taste
- 2 cups nonfat milk
- 10 oz. spinach, chopped
- 2 cups cooked brown rice
- 2 cups cooked turkey, chopped
- 2 oz. Parmesan cheese

Instructions:

1. In pan over medium heat, cook the onion, garlic, sweet pepper and mushrooms in butter.

2. Add the flour, thyme, salt and pepper.

3. Gradually add the milk.

4. Mix until thick and bubbly.

5. Add the rice, spinach, turkey and half of the Parmesan cheese.

6. Spread the mixture into a baking pan.

7. Top with the remaining cheese.

8. Bake in the oven for 20 minutes.

9. Uncover and bake for another 10 minutes.

Nutrients per Serving:

- Calories 287
- Fat 8 g
- Saturated fat 3 g
- Carbohydrates 28 g
- Fiber 3 g
- Protein 24 g
- Cholesterol 53 mg
- Sugars 6 g
- Sodium 393 mg
- Potassium 775 mg

Chicken Strata

Layers of chicken, mushrooms, sweet peppers, asparagus, egg and Swiss cheese create this decadent casserole dish that will surely become your favorite.

Serving Size: 6

Preparation Cooking Time: 35 minutes

Ingredients:

- 1 tablespoon vegetable oil
- 2 cups asparagus, sliced
- 1 ½ cups fresh mushrooms, sliced
- ½ cup red sweet pepper, chopped
- Cooking spray
- 4 cups English muffins, sliced into smaller pieces
- 10 oz. chicken breast, cooked and shredded
- 3 oz. Swiss cheese, shredded
- 1 cup nonfat milk
- 4 eggs, beaten
- Pepper to taste

Instructions:

1. Preheat your oven to 325 degrees F.

2. In pan over medium heat, cook the mushrooms, sweet pepper and asparagus for 3 minutes.

3. Spray your muffin pan with oil.

4. Place half of the muffin pieces in the muffin cups.

5. Top with half of the cheese, asparagus mixture and cooked chicken.

6. Add the remaining muffin pieces on top.

7. In a bowl, mix the milk, eggs and pepper.

8. Pour the mixture into the muffin cups.

9. Sprinkle with the remaining cheese. Bake for 30 minutes.

10. Let cool for 10 minutes before serving.

Nutrients per Serving:

- Calories 243
- Fat 7.9 g
- Saturated fat 2.8 g
- Carbohydrates 21.7 g
- Fiber 3.7 g
- Protein 23.1 g
- Cholesterol 35 mg
- Sugars 8 g
- Sodium 777 mg
- Potassium 393 mg

Chicken Cashew Casserole

An Asian inspired recipe that combines colorful vegetables, brown rice, chow-mein noodles and cashews—this dish is expected to impress your family and friends.

Serving Size: 6

Preparation Cooking Time: 1 hour

Ingredients:

- Cooking spray
- ¼ cup hoisin sauce
- 1 cup low-sodium chicken broth
- 4 teaspoons cornstarch
- 2 tablespoons freshly grated ginger
- Pepper to taste
- ½ teaspoon red pepper flakes
- 1 lb. chicken breast fillet, sliced into strips
- 2 onions, sliced into wedges
- 6 cloves garlic, crushed and minced
- ½ cup cashews
- 2 stalks celery, sliced
- 1 green sweet pepper, chopped
- 1 cup chow-mein noodles, coarsely broken
- 2 cups bok choy, sliced
- 2 carrots, sliced
- 2 cups brown rice, cooked
- ¼ cup green onions, chopped

Instructions:

1. Preheat your oven to 400 degrees F.

2. Spray your baking pan with oil.

3. In a bowl, mix the hoisin sauce, chicken broth, cornstarch, ginger, pepper and red pepper flakes. Set aside.

4. Spray your pan with oil.

5. Put it over medium heat.

6. Cook the chicken until brown on both sides.

7. Transfer to a plate.

8. Add the onions, garlic, celery, sweet pepper, bok choy and carrots in the pan.

9. Cook for 4 minutes.

10. Pour in the sauce.

11. Cook for 3 minutes.

12. Put your chicken back to the pan along with the cooked rice.

13. Transfer the mixture to the baking pan.

14. Cover with foil.

15. Bake for 20 minutes.

16. Remove the foil.

17. Sprinkle the cashews and noodles on top.

18. Bake for another 5 minutes.

19. Garnish with the green onions and serve.

Nutrients per Serving:

- Calories 340
- Fat 10.1 g
- Saturated fat 2.2 g
- Carbohydrates 40.4 g
- Fiber 4.2 g
- Protein 22.9 g
- Cholesterol 49 mg
- Sugars 8 g
- Sodium 480 mg
- Potassium 718 mg

Baked Tomato Squash

This casserole dish is not only full of color but also loaded with exciting flavors as well as essential nutrients. Baked squash, zucchini and tomato slices are topped with pine nut gremolata to create an unforgettable dish everyone will rave about.

Serving Size: 6

Preparation Cooking Time: an hour and 30 minutes

Ingredients:

Sauce

- 3 cloves garlic, sliced in half
- 12 oz. roasted red sweet peppers
- 8 oz. unsalted tomato sauce
- ¼ teaspoon red pepper flakes
- 1 ½ teaspoons dried Italian seasoning

Vegetables

- 1 lb. squash, sliced
- 1 ½ lb. tomatoes, sliced and cored
- 1 zucchini, sliced

Pine Nut Gremolata

- ½ cup fresh basil leaves, sliced thinly
- ¼ cup low-fat feta cheese, crumbled
- ¼ cup pine nuts, toasted and chopped
- 1 teaspoon freshly grated lemon zest

Instructions:

1. Preheat your oven to 375 degrees F.

2. Add the garlic, sweet peppers, tomato sauce, red pepper flakes and Italian seasoning in the blender.

3. Pulse until smooth.

4. Pour the sauce on top of a baking pan.

5. Layer the squash, tomatoes and zucchinis in the baking pan.

6. Bake for 45 minutes.

7. Combine the gremolata ingredients.

8. Sprinkle this on top of the baked vegetables before serving.

Nutrients per Serving:

- Calories 109
- Fat 5.2 g
- Saturated fat 0.9 g
- Carbohydrates 12.8 g
- Fiber 3.9 g
- Protein 4.9 g
- Cholesterol 2 mg
- Sugars 8 g
- Sodium 206 mg
- Potassium 646 mg

Burger Casserole

There are too many things that you will be falling for about this recipe. Not only is this full of delicious flavors, it's also healthier compared to the classic hamburger casserole. This one is made with ground turkey, fewer potatoes but includes more vegetables.

Serving Size: 4

Preparation Cooking Time: 1 hour and 10 minutes

Ingredients:

- 1 parsnip, sliced
- 2 potatoes, sliced into wedges
- ¼ cup low-fat yogurt
- Salt to taste
- ½ cup onion, chopped
- 12 oz. ground turkey
- ¼ cup water
- 16 oz. frozen mixed vegetables
- ¼ cup tomato paste (unsalted)
- Pepper to taste
- 15 oz. stewed tomatoes
- 1 tablespoon Worcestershire sauce
- 1 teaspoon dried sage

Instructions:

1. Preheat your oven to 375 degrees F.

2. In a pan over medium high heat, boil the parsnip and potatoes in water for 20 minutes.

3. Drain.

4. Mash the parsnip and potatoes using a fork or potato masher.

5. Stir in the yogurt and salt.

6. Continue mashing.

7. Cover with foil to keep warm.

8. In pan over medium heat, cook the onion and turkey for 3 to 5 minutes.

9. Drain the fat.

10. Add the mixed veggies and water into the pan.

11. Cover the pan and simmer for 8 minutes.

12. Stir in the rest of the ingredients.

13. Heat for 2 minutes.

14. Pour the mixture into a baking pan.

15. Spread the mashed potatoes on top.

16. Bake in the oven for 20 minutes.

Nutrients per Serving:

- Calories 279
- Fat 2 g
- Saturated fat 1 g
- Carbohydrates 41 g
- Fiber 7 g
- Protein 25 g
- Cholesterol 35 mg
- Sugars 1 g
- Sodium 287 mg
- Potassium 550 mg

Pizza Casserole

This is a different way of making pizza casserole. Included in the dish are slices of summer squash, sweet pepper, mushrooms and onions. Instead of ground beef, this recipe uses ground turkey.

Serving Size: 6

Preparation Cooking Time: 1 hour

Ingredients:

- 1 cup onion, chopped
- 1 cup green sweet pepper, chopped
- 2 cups mushrooms, sliced
- 1 ½ cups summer squash, chopped
- 1 ¼ lb. ground turkey
- 15 oz. pizza sauce
- 1 teaspoon dried Italian seasoning
- ½ teaspoon fennel seeds, crushed
- 2 eggs
- 1 cup nonfat milk
- 1 tablespoon vegetable oil
- 1 cup all-purpose flour
- 4 oz. low-fat mozzarella cheese
- 2 tablespoons Parmesan cheese, grated

Instructions:

1. Preheat your oven to 400 degrees F.

2. In a pan, cook the onion, sweet pepper, mushrooms, squash and ground turkey for 5 to 7 minutes, stirring frequently.

3. Drain the fat.

4. Add the pizza sauce.

5. Season with the fennel seeds and Italian seasoning.

6. Bring to a boil.

7. Reduce heat and simmer for 5 minutes.

8. Spread into the baking pan.

9. In a bowl, beat the eggs, milk and oil using an electric mixer set of medium speed.

10. Beat for 1 minute.

11. Stir in the flour.

12. Beat for 1 more minute.

13. Sprinkle mozzarella cheese on top of the skillet.

14. Pour the egg mixture on top.

15. Sprinkle Parmesan cheese on top of the egg mixture.

16. Bake in the oven for 30 minutes.

17. Serve warm.

Nutrients per Serving:

- Calories 327
- Fat 7 g
- Saturated fat 2 g
- Carbohydrates 31 g
- Fiber 3 g
- Protein 34 g
- Cholesterol 58 mg
- Sugars 7 g
- Sodium 611 mg
- Potassium 766 mg

Chicken Curry Casserole

This recipe can be done in various ways. Instead of chicken, you can also use turkey or pork. You can also add vegetables available in your kitchen.

Serving Size: 2

Preparation Cooking Time: 20 minutes

Ingredients:

- Cooking spray
- ¼ cup onion, chopped
- 1 teaspoon curry powder
- 5 oz. chicken breast, cooked and sliced into cubes
- ¼ cup frozen peas
- ⅔ cup water
- ¼ cup low-fat mayonnaise
- ¼ cup quick-cooking couscous
- ¼ cup red sweet pepper, chopped
- 2 tablespoons mango chutney

Instructions:

1. Spray your heat proof bowls with oil. Set aside.

2. Preheat your pan over medium heat.

3. Cook the onion for 2 minutes.

4. Add the curry powder and cook while stirring for 1 minute.

5. Pour in the water and add the couscous.

6. Increase heat to medium high and bring to a boil.

7. Add the rest of the ingredients.

8. Pour the mixture into the bowls and serve.

Nutrients per Serving:

- Calories 303
- Fat 3.3 g
- Saturated fat 0.8 g
- Carbohydrates 39.3 g
- Fiber 3.1 g
- Protein 27.3 g
- Cholesterol 59 mg
- Sugars 6 g
- Sodium 365 mg
- Potassium 442 mg

Pasta Casserole

Pasta casseroles are quick and easy to make, even with long cooking hours. In this recipe, we make one using multi-grain penne smothered with delicious Italian sauce and topped with melted cheese.

Serving Size: 8

Preparation Cooking Time: 1 hour and 10 minutes

Ingredients:

- 8 oz. multi-grain penne pasta
- 1 onion, chopped
- 2 cloves garlic, crushed and minced
- 1 cup mushrooms, chopped
- 1 sweet red pepper, chopped
- 12 oz. ground Italian turkey sausage
- 1 cup zucchini, chopped
- 8 oz. unsalted tomato sauce
- 15 oz. canned diced tomatoes
- 1 tablespoon dried basil
- 1 teaspoon dried oregano
- Salt and pepper to taste
- 4 oz. low-fat Italian blend cheese

Instructions:

1. Preheat your oven to 350 degrees F.

2. Prepare your pasta according to the directions in the package but skip the oil and salt.

3. Drain. Set aside on a plate.

4. In pan over medium heat, cook the onion, garlic, mushrooms, sweet pepper, zucchini and sausage.

5. Drain the fat.

6. Stir in the tomato sauce and tomatoes.

7. Season with the salt, pepper, dried oregano and dried basil.

8. Bring to a boil.

9. Reduce heat and simmer for 10 minutes.

10. Transfer the sausage mixture to a baking pan.

11. Stir in the pasta.

12. Bake for 40 minutes.

13. Sprinkle the cheese on top.

14. Bake lastly for another 5 minutes or until the cheese has melted.

Nutrients per Serving:

- Calories 254
- Fat 7.1 g
- Saturated fat 2.7 g
- Carbohydrates 30.1 g
- Fiber 3.2 g
- Protein 16.8 g
- Cholesterol 2 mg
- Sugars 6 g
- Sodium 492 mg
- Potassium 291 mg

Sausage Sweet Potato Casserole

One look at this dish and you know it won't disappoint. What makes this casserole extra special is the sprinkling of crumbled goat cheese on top.

Serving Size: 8

Preparation Cooking Time: 1 hour and 20 minutes

Ingredients:

- Cooking spray
- 6 oz. turkey sausage
- 1 cup onion, chopped
- 4 cloves garlic, crushed and minced
- 1 cup red sweet pepper, chopped
- 1 tablespoon water
- 1 teaspoon olive oil
- 5 oz. baby spinach
- 1 ½ cups sweet potatoes, roasted
- 8 eggs, beaten
- 4 egg whites
- ½ cup nonfat milk
- ½ teaspoon dry mustard
- ½ teaspoon red pepper flakes
- Salt and pepper to taste
- 2 tablespoons green onion, chopped
- 2 oz. goat cheese, crumbled

Instructions:

1. Preheat your oven to 350 degrees F.

2. Spray your baking pan with oil.

3. In pan over medium heat, cook the sausage for 6 minutes, stirring frequently.

4. Drain the fat.

5. In the same pan, add the garlic, onion and sweet pepper.

6. Cook for 7 minutes.

7. Pour in the water.

8. Scrape the browned bits using a wooden spoon.

9. Stir in the spinach and cook for 2 minutes.

10. Add the sweet potatoes and sausage.

11. Mix well. Transfer the mixture to a baking pan.

12. In a bowl, beat eggs and egg whites.

13. Stir in the milk and season with the mustard, red pepper flakes, salt and pepper.

14. Pour this mixture over the sausages.

15. Bake in the oven for 40 minutes.

16. Sprinkle with the green onion and goat cheese before serving.

Nutrients per Serving:

- Calories 219
- Fat 11.4 g
- Saturated fat 4 g
- Carbohydrates 11.9 g
- Fiber 2.2 g
- Protein 17 g
- Cholesterol 215 mg
- Sugars 4 g
- Sodium 446 mg
- Potassium 313 mg

Hash Brown Baked Eggs

This casserole dish is actually easier than it looks. Create this when you want to serve something special to your family but don't want to take too much time in the kitchen.

Serving Size: 8

Preparation Cooking Time: 50 minutes

Ingredients:

- Cooking spray
- 20 oz. hash brown potatoes, shredded
- 1 tablespoon olive oil
- 1 green sweet pepper, sliced into thick rings
- ½ cup pizza sauce
- 1 oz. Parmesan cheese, shredded
- 8 eggs
- Pepper to taste

Instructions:

1. Preheat your oven to 365 degrees F.

2. Spray your baking pan with oil.

3. Add the potatoes and drizzle with the oil.

4. Toss to coat evenly.

5. Spread the potatoes in your baking pan.

6. Bake in the oven for 10 minutes.

7. Stir and bake for another 10 minutes.

8. Arrange the pepper rings on top of the potatoes.

9. Spread pizza sauce inside each of the pepper rings.

10. Break the eggs into the pepper rings.

11. Top each one with the Parmesan cheese.

12. Bake for 15 minutes.

13. Season with the pepper before serving.

Nutrients per Serving:

- Calories 179
- Fat 7.2 g
- Saturated fat 2.2 g
- Carbohydrates 17.9 g
- Fiber 2.4 g
- Protein 9.4 g
- Cholesterol 188 mg
- Sugars 2 g
- Sodium 491 mg
- Potassium 106 mg

Conclusion

As what this book has proved, casseroles are not that difficult to prepare.

Simply chop and slice, throw it all into the baking pan and bake for a few minutes, and that's it.

Of course, sometimes, you'd have to brown the meat first or sauté it with onion and garlic to make the dish tastier.

But overall, preparations are minimal.

Even with little effort, the results are outstanding.

Are you ready to get started in the kitchen?

About the Author

A native of Albuquerque, New Mexico, Sophia Freeman found her calling in the culinary arts when she enrolled at the Sante Fe School of Cooking. Freeman decided to take a year after graduation and travel around Europe, sampling the cuisine from small bistros and family owned restaurants from Italy to Portugal. Her bubbly personality and inquisitive nature made her popular with the locals in the villages and when she finished her trip and came home, she had made friends for life in the places she had visited. She also came home with a deeper understanding of European cuisine.

Freeman went to work at one of Albuquerque's 5-star restaurants as a sous-chef and soon worked her way up to head chef. The restaurant began to feature Freeman's original dishes as specials on the menu and soon after, she began to write e-books with her recipes. Sophia's dishes mix local flavours with European inspiration making them irresistible to the diners in her restaurant and the online community.

Freeman's experience in Europe didn't just teach her new ways of cooking, but also unique methods of presentation. Using rich sauces, crisp vegetables and meat cooked to perfection, she creates a stunning display as well as a delectable dish. She has won many local awards for her cuisine and she continues to delight her diners with her culinary masterpieces.

* * * ★ ★ ★ ★ ★ ★ ★ * *

Author's Afterthoughts

I want to convey my big thanks to all of my readers who have taken the time to read my book. Readers like you make my work so rewarding and I cherish each and every one of you.

Grateful cannot describe how I feel when I know that someone has chosen my work over all of the choices available online. I hope you enjoyed the book as much as I enjoyed writing it.

Feedback from my readers is how I grow and learn as a chef and an author. Please take the time to let me know your thoughts by leaving a review on Amazon so I and your fellow readers can learn from your experience.

My deepest thanks,

Sophia Freeman

Subscribe to the Newsletter!

https://sophia.subscribemenow.com/

★ ★ ★ ★ ★ ★ ★ ★ ★ ★ ★ ★

Printed in Dunstable, United Kingdom